THE
NEXT
DAY

THE NEXT DAY
A Journey with Jesus
in the 40 Days After Easter

By Larry L. Thompson

www.TheNextDayBook.com

Published by Larry Thompson Ministries and Michael Thomas Group

All rights reserved. Except for brief excerpts for review purposes, no part of this book may be reproduced or used in any form without written permission from the publisher.

All other Scripture quotations, unless otherwise noted, are taken from the Holy Bible, New Living Translation, Copyright 1996. Used by permission of Tyndale House Publishers, Inc., Wheaton, Illinois 60189.

Scripture quotations from THE MESSAGE. Copyright © by Eugene H. Peterson 1993, 1994, 1995, 1996, 2000, 2001, 2002. Used by permission of Tyndale House Publishers, Inc.

Scripture quotations marked NIV are taken from the Holy Bible, New International Version®. NIV®. Copyright © 1973, 1978, 1984 by International Bible Society. Used by permission of Zondervan.

Visit our website at www.LarryThompson.org for more resources like these.

ISBN: 978-0-692-40414-0

©2015 Larry Thompson

Lead Editor: Mike Jeffries
Editing Team: Tina Anderson, Bridget Jeffries, Mary Springer

Printed in the United States of America
First Edition 2015
2 3 4 5 6 7 8 9 10 11

THE NEXT DAY
A Journey with Jesus
in the 40 Days After Easter

Larry L. Thompson

Preface to
The Next Day

If you were to pick any random day in your life, chances are pretty good you would have no memory what exactly you were doing on that day. However, if you were to ask someone what they were doing on the morning of September 11, 2001, they could immediately tell you in detail. They would not remember what happened September 10, 2001...but the NEXT DAY...they will never forget.

All of us can associate dates and facts readily when there has been a "NEXT DAY" that has been indelibly recorded in our life.

I can't remember anything I did on August 17, 1972...but ask me about the NEXT DAY and I can remember almost every detail. The most beautiful woman in the world walked down the aisle of our church and Cynthia became my wife!

I don't remember much about November 13, 1976, but the NEXT DAY...I can't even describe the joy of being introduced to our first daughter. We named her Ami but after 5,475 days of sharing our life with her, I remember when she changed her name to Taylor! I like Taylor...but then again, I liked Ami! Mostly I just love that girl.

Speaking of girls, not sure what we did on July 24, 1979, but I will never forget the NEXT DAY. Anticipating an easy delivery, the birth of our second daughter turned into a nightmare. Thank God, what could have been a tragedy turned that NEXT DAY into a victory and we continue to experience the joy of Jennifer's life.

I continue to have many NEXT DAY family moments in my life, receiving my new sons by marriage (Mason and Martin) and then welcoming two grandsons, Strong and Tru. They delight Cynthia and I as we imagine the future their own next days will bring.

But as great as those Next Days were, one was even greater. Just over two thousand years ago.

That's when three women experienced the greatest NEXT DAY the world has ever known. Mark describes the NEXT DAY this way:

Very early, **the next day***, on Sunday morning, just at sunrise, they went to the tomb. On the way they were asking each other, "Who will roll away the stone for us from the entrance to the tomb?"*

But as they arrived, they looked up and saw that the stone, which was very large, had already been rolled aside. When they entered the tomb, they saw a young man clothed in a white robe sitting on the right side.

The women were shocked, but the angel said, "Don't be alarmed. You are looking for Jesus of Nazareth, who was crucified. He isn't here! He is risen from the dead! Look, this is where they laid His body.
(Mark 16:3-6)

Had there never been a NEXT DAY, had Jesus never been resurrected, think of the enormous impact it would have on our world.

If there is no NEXT DAY, Jesus would still be in the tomb. Few would ever know about Him. His life would be nothing more than a sentence in history. We would have to tear down all the churches and cathedrals all around the world. We would need to destroy some of mankind's greatest architecture.

If there is not a NEXT DAY, then Michelangelo's Sistine Chapel would never have been the masterpiece it is today. We would have no Last Supper by DaVinci. We would be without Handel's Messiah. We would have also been without the music of Johann Sebastian Bach, who dedicated every note he wrote to the glory of God.

Dante, Donne, Dickens and Dostoyevsky all drew their ink from the diverse and deep well of the life of Jesus, the principles He taught and the NEXT DAY He lived.

William Shakespeare is even said to have translated a portion of the Bible. (Look in Psalm 46, 46 words in and 46 words from the end, to see what is thought to be his secret signature.)

One of the things I love about living in South Florida, and especially our church, is that we are a multicultural, multiracial fellowship. Think about the impact of the NEXT DAY in regards to civil rights. Because of the NEXT DAY on that Easter Sunday morning two thousand years ago, great Christians like William Wilberforce and Dr. Martin Luther King, Jr. dedicated their lives to provide equality and equal rights to all people.

Indeed, the very national fabric which allowed such freedoms was made possible by the NEXT DAY that inspired liberty in leaders like George Washington, John Adams, John Hancock, Alexander Hamilton and Patrick Henry.

The printing press was invented by a NEXT DAY Christian named Johann Gutenberg so he could put Bibles in the hands of the people. The greatest universities, including nearly every college in Europe and on the new continent, were founded by followers of Jesus.

If there had not been a NEXT DAY, the greatest scientists would have been without their highest calling. Scientists and physicians who enlightened our understanding of God's perfect order include Copernicus, Gallileo Gallilei, Blaise Pascal, Johann Kepler and Isaac Newton.

With the NEXT DAY came compassion and care the world had never seen before. Children abandoned on the streets were adopted by Next Day believers. The first hospitals were built by followers of Jesus who understood that healing comes from the hand of God. Pioneering doctors and modern researchers like Walter Reed and Francis Collins (who directs the National Institute of Health and decoded the human genome) followed the Great Physician.

Even today, the three largest crisis emergency organizations (the Red Cross, the Salvation Army and Baptist Disaster Relief) exist because their humanitarian organizers believed in the NEXT DAY.

One writer goes as far as to say, "Every time that charity and compassion are seen in operation, the credit goes to Jesus Christ. It is He who inspired his early followers to give and to help the unfortunate, regardless of their race, religion, class or nationality."[1]

However, the most important difference that the NEXT DAY can make is the difference the NEXT DAY can make in your life.

This book would be meaningless and a waste of your time had there been no NEXT DAY for Jesus.

There would be no celebration of the day before the NEXT DAY that we know as Easter Sunday! If there is not a NEXT DAY, then there is no resurrection and all that is done in His name is useless. Paul reminded us just how important the NEXT DAY is to all of us: *"And if Christ has not been raised, then all our preaching is useless, and your faith is useless."* 1 Corinthians 15:14 (NLT)

I am so thankful that there was a NEXT DAY and there is HOPE because of Jesus. I would like to invite you to join me as we look at the 40 NEXT DAYS following the miraculous events of Easter Sunday. After each day's devotional, I have provided you the space to write your thoughts and create your own journal as you walk through these Next Days with Christ.

We will be inspired by His life, and as He prepared His disciples to change the world, and it is my prayer that Christ would prepare us to live each day in light and anticipation of the eternal value of the NEXT DAY.

Dr. Larry Thompson
Fort Lauderdale, Florida
Easter 2015

40 Days with Jesus After Easter Sunday

THE NEXT DAY

Appears to Mary of Magdala
(John 20:11-18)

Appears to His mother, Mary, and three others
(Mark 16, Matthew 28, Luke 24:10)

Appears to Peter
(Luke 24:34. I Corinthians 15:5)

Appears to two travelers on the Road to Emmaus
(Luke 24:13-35)

First visit to ten of the disciples (all except Thomas)
(John 20:19-25, Luke 24:36-43)

THE SECOND, THIRD, AND FOURTH WEEKS

Second appearance to disciples (and now Thomas)
(John 20:26-29)

Appears to some of the disciples at the Sea of Galilee
(John 21)

Appears to the disciples and at least 500 others
(I Corinthians 15:6, Matthew 28:16-17)

Appears to His brother, James
(I Corinthians 15:7)

40 DAYS AFTER EASTER

Final appearance to disciples and other followers in Jerusalem just before the Ascension
(Acts 1:3-11, Luke 24:49-53)

Three days ago. Such a short time.

Short yes, but also truly, absolutely, incontrovertibly an eternity.

Not only for Jesus, who redefined eternity in those seventy-two hours, but also for those who spent three years walking with Him, laughing with Him, crying for Him.

Three days ago darkness. Now yesterday, light so bright that it shattered tombstone and raised the dead.

Which brings us to today. **The next day....**

Day 1

"Surprise!"

Luke 24:1-3

"But very early on Sunday morning the women went to the tomb, taking the spices they had prepared. 2 They found that the stone had been rolled away from the entrance. 3 So they went in, but they didn't find the body of the Lord Jesus." Luke 24:1-3 (NLT)

When our daughter Jennifer was approaching her eighth birthday, she informed us she wanted a "Surprise Birthday Party." She went on to tell us everything she wanted and the guests she wanted us to invite and to be sure it was a "surprise!" I would like to say that this was the only year that Jen asked for a surprise party but the pattern continued for many years. Now, history repeats itself and Jen's son, our six-year old grandson, announced, "I want to have a surprise birthday party this year!"

Talk about a real surprise…Go back to the first Easter Sunday. Early that morning, women went to the grave where Jesus had been buried. They had worried about how they would roll the stone away that sealed the entrance to the tomb and yet when they arrived, they found that the stone had been rolled away already. FIRST SURPRISE! The entrance to the grave was empty. SECOND SURPRISE! They wondered what had happened to Jesus.

While they were wondering about this, suddenly, two men in dazzling bright clothes appeared to the two women. THIRD SURPRISE! Now, when angels suddenly appear and start talking to you the situation moves from SURPRISE to "LET'S GET THE HECK OUT OF DODGE!" The men spoke to the women and said, "Why are you looking for the living among the dead? Jesus is not here, He has risen just as he told you he would." FOURTH SURPRISE!

Suddenly, the women at the empty tomb remembered, the SURPRISE of the empty tomb had been discussed by Jesus long before the PARTY! They were no longer surprised, instead they ran back to remind the disciples: "Hurry, come to the tomb, the SURPRISE PARTY has started…" And it continues every day someone is surprised when they discover the Living Christ has brought them an eternal gift…the gift of eternal life.

YOUR NEXT DAY: Today, write your thoughts about the day you were "surprised" when Jesus came into your life. If you have never been "surprised" by Christ, then pray that He would surprise you by revealing to your life that He is the Risen Savior.

Day 1

NOTES about your Next Day

> Talk about a real surprise…
> Go back to the first Easter Sunday.

Day 2

"Mary, Mary, How Does Your Garden Grow?"

John 20:14-16

My grandmother had a magnificent garden in her backyard. Every year she would meticulously weed her garden, plant the seeds, fertilize the garden and then wait for the glorious beauty to be revealed every spring. One of the great joys of her life was sharing the beauty of her garden with others.

Cynthia and I tried the garden thing...ONCE. We planted potatoes and I guess we got carried away because we had a "bountiful" harvest. As a matter of record, we had so many potatoes that we had to store them in the garage and couldn't even get the cars inside because of all the spuds. We gave away what we could but I never got so fed up with something so mashed, baked, scalloped, chopped, fried and julienned.

It is not by accident that Jesus visited two gardens the weekend of His death and resurrection. The first garden was the Garden of Gethsemane where the Savior experienced the greatest trial of His life. If the enemy could have destroyed the life in that Garden we would have never been introduced to the second Garden, because the gate to get into the second garden required going to the cross.

She turned to leave and saw someone standing there. It was Jesus, but she didn't recognize him. "Dear woman, why are you crying?" Jesus asked her. "Who are you looking for?" She thought he was the gardener. "Sir," she said, "if you have taken him away, tell me where you have put him, and I will go and get him." "Mary!" Jesus said. She turned to him and cried out, "Rabboni!" John 20:14-16 (NLT)

After the cross, Jesus was placed in a borrowed tomb located in the midst of the beautiful garden of life. Just as there came a time every year when the glorious beauty of my grandmother's flowers would spring forth from the ground, Jesus rose from death in liberation as the Promised Messiah.

Today, the beauty that came forth from the garden tomb continues to bring joy and hope to all who receive Him. Such a difference between the two gardens...one a garden of surrender and the other the garden of salvation.

YOUR NEXT DAY: What are you facing today that appears to be so powerful and so strong that you almost anticipate total defeat in your life? Take a moment and revisit the two Gardens of Christ...you may be surprised by what blooms in this time with Him today!

Day 2

NOTES about your Next Day

Day 3

"Desperate Brevity"

Matthew 26:39

I have been in thousands of prayer meetings in my life. Some have lasted for a few hours, others only a few minutes, but I have always found the most urgent, the most dependent, the most critical prayers are those that are uttered with desperate brevity.

Our youngest daughter was a senior in high school and she had travelled with her boyfriend's parents to Virginia. It was a Saturday afternoon and I had come home from the office with a migraine headache. The phone rang and I heard my wife scream "Who is this?" I grabbed the phone and a man said, "I am in Virginia and on the highway and there has been a terrible accident and your daughter is in the car. She is alive but I'm not sure about the other three people." He then held the phone up to my daughter so she could talk to me. From the rolled-over car, my daughter screamed, "Daddy, come quick!" and the phone went silent. We had no idea where she was and we couldn't get a plane out to Virginia until the next day. I called the private jet service and we used our savings to fly as fast as we could to get to her. Though the accident seriously injured our friends, they all lived and we share that praise today. However, what I'll never forget is the cry of my daughter, "Daddy, come quick!"

As we reflect on the miracle of Easter and the resurrection of Jesus Christ, it is important that we remember how Matthew describes the words of our Savior, and one of the shortest prayers in the bible.

"My Father! If it is possible, let this cup of suffering be taken away from Me. Yet I want your will to be done, not Mine." Matthew 26:39b (NLT)

I love the fact that Satan didn't throw Jesus to the ground in fear like a coward, but Jesus knelt like the Hero He is. He went through the human suffering that we would all experience and took that pain, ridicule, mocking and ultimate death so that He could not only relate to us but provide salvation for us. Truly, courage is not the absence of fear but the conquest of fear.

YOUR NEXT DAY: What is there in your life that has the power to destroy you and yet all God is waiting for is to hear you say, "Your will be done, not mine."

Day 3

NOTES about your Next Day

Day 4

"Secret Followers"

John 19:38-42

Afterward Joseph of Arimathea, who had been a secret disciple of Jesus (because he feared the Jewish leaders), asked Pilate for permission to take down Jesus' body. When Pilate gave permission, Joseph came and took the body away. With him came Nicodemus, the man who had come to Jesus at night. He brought seventy-five pounds of perfumed ointment made from myrrh and aloes. Following Jewish burial custom, they wrapped Jesus' body with the spices in long sheets of linen cloth. John 19:38-40 (NLT)

In biblical days, it was the custom that the family of the deceased was obligated to care for the body. Amazingly, John tells us that two secret disciples stepped forward from their hiding and boldly asked Pilate for the responsibility to prepare the body of Jesus. Joseph and Nicodemus are two men that you would never have believed would be the ones to honor the man they had grown to love and respect as their Messiah.

We know both men were prominent and religious and yet chose that day a relationship over their religion. Of all the hundreds and thousands of people Jesus had met and ministered to over the three years, only two stepped out of the shadows to take their stand.

I love what Edwin Blum wrote about these two secret servants: "Joseph and Nicodemus' act of love and respect for the body of Jesus was for them dangerous, costly, and without personal gain. The service of Christians for their living Lord should be equally courageous and sacrificial, for our labor is not in vain."

As I think back through my life, I recall several "secret disciples" who stepped up. I remember one young man in college by the name of Gary who carried a giant Bible everywhere he went. I heard people ridicule him and while I was a Christian, I remained in the shadows, as a secret follower, rather than take a stand for Gary and the Savior he loved. Even though other Christians have also hidden in fear of what this world would say if they spoke the truth of scripture, God has always had a "Gary or Joseph or Nicodemus" ready to step out of the shadows into the Light of His grace, and without apology take their stand to honor the life of Jesus Christ.

YOUR NEXT DAY: In what areas have you been a "secret disciple?" What can you do today to come out of the shadows and proudly take your stand for the One who gave His life for you?

Day 4

NOTES about your Next Day

Day 5

"I am with you always"
Luke 8:1-3

People have often asked why Mary of Magdala was alone when she went to the tomb. It most likely was because of her reputation. Mary is a woman from the Galilean town of Magdala. Luke tells us that Jesus healed her of seven demons that had tormented her for years. (Luke 8:1-3) She became one of the leading ladies who supported the ministry of Jesus by giving Him offerings from her possessions. We know from Scripture that Mary Magdala followed Jesus without fear and without apology. She was bold and she was brave. She was also a wealthy woman who had a very difficult life until Jesus brought her peace and comfort. She then spent the rest of her life as a committed believer that used her resources to help the Messiah take His message to the world.

I have a very dear friend by the name of Celia. She is to me, a modern-day Mary Magdala. Life was difficult for her as a young mother of two young children who one day felt she was on top of the world, married to a wonderful surgeon who owned and operated a hospital…and the next day, seeing the love of her life lose his battle to cancer.

Without question, Satan attempted to torment and lie to her about what life would be like in the future. However, like Mary Magdala, Celia took life one day at a time, each day looking for Jesus and each day hearing His same gentle response He gave to Mary, "Celia, I am with you always." Celia is a woman who would tell you immediately, "If you're looking for Jesus…He will find you." Once Jesus has found us, our lives are just a postscript thanking Him for His grace and looking for opportunities to invest in His work so others will know Him.

Can you imagine the joy that was Mary's? She was the very FIRST person to see the Resurrected Savior! The lady, who was once tormented by pain, is now filled with passion and she has the joy to be the first to tell the world, "I have seen the Lord!"

YOUR NEXT DAY: Many of us can recall the times we cried out to Jesus and He met our need. But can we also claim to have the testimony of Mary Magdala and Celia? Have we told the world, "I was looking for Jesus and He found me?" Have we honored Jesus with our life as our way of saying, "Thank you, Jesus for all you have done for me"? Ask the Lord to show you someone today that you can bless because Christ has first blessed you!

Day 5

NOTES about your Next Day

Day 6

"Why Are You Crying?"
John 20:15-16

Just about everyone has been "lost in grief" at some point in your life. Many times through the past 40 years, I have sat with friends and loved ones who have been lost in grief. The pain of some tragic accident, unexpected illness or rejection by someone you love has driven us to our knees. I have wiped tears away with a wet washcloth and held adults and children as their grief overwhelmed the very room we were in. I silently prayed. "Jesus, I know You are present, I ask You to make yourself known and bring some relief to this broken heart." Eventually, God's Spirit would minister to the broken-hearted...eventually.

You see, many of us are like Mary of Magdala, who couldn't believe what she had just seen happen to Jesus. We are lost in our grief, overwhelmed with hurt and pain. It seems almost insensitive to ask, "Why are you crying?" But this is a question that must be asked. At some point we must push through the tears that cloud our vision and hear Jesus call us by name. Just like Mary did.

"Dear woman, why are you crying?" Jesus asked her. "Who are you looking for?" She thought he was the gardener. "Sir," she said, "if you have taken him away, tell me where you have put him, and I will go and get him." "Mary!" Jesus said. She turned to him and cried out, "Rabboni!" (which is Hebrew for "Teacher"). John 20:15-16 (NLT)

There is something very personal about our name and something even more powerful when our name is spoken by the Risen Savior. Jesus was standing right in front of her and yet she did not realize it was Him. That is what pain and grief do to our emotional and spiritual life. Finally, Jesus said ONE WORD that changed everything. Jesus called her by NAME... "MARY!"

YOUR NEXT DAY: Pray today for those who are in such painful grief that, even though they are Christian, they are finding it very difficult to see the glorious Savior who stands with them in the midst of their pain. Write their name down. Pray for them. Call them. Write them a note and remind them who is with them...even though they may be lost in their grief.

Day 6

NOTES about your Next Day

> There is something very personal about our name and something even more powerful when our name is spoken by the Risen Savior.

Day 7

"From Emotion to Motion"

John 20:17-18

Jesus said, "For I haven't yet ascended to the Father. But go find my brothers and tell them that I am ascending to my Father and your Father, to my God and your God." Mary Magdalene found the disciples and told them, "I have seen the Lord!" Then she gave them His message." John 20:17b-18 (NLT)

Think about this: Mary Magdalene has been misunderstood by history and questioned because of irresponsible journalism and yet SHE WAS THE FIRST TO SEE THE RESURRECTED SAVIOR! I would go so far as to say she took the power of the resurrection and went from emotion to motion! Jesus said, "GO FIND MY BROTHERS AND TELL THEM..."

Peter and John had visited the same tomb and had left despondent, thinking someone had stolen the body. They return home, and there is no fanfare. We've all been there, feeling only distance between the hope and love that God promised and our own doubt or despair. Gail O'Day writes this about those first disciples: "Until the community encounters the risen Jesus, there are no categories through which to understand the empty tomb. The pre-resurrection world cannot make sense of an empty tomb with any theory except grave robbing"

All through Mary's life she was searching for Jesus. Once He changed her life and delivered her from torment, she was committed to honoring Him. Her search at the tomb does not surprise me. Her response to the Master does not surprise me. The message that transformed Mary from emotion to motion continues to be shouted by the Spirit into our hearts this very day. "Go and tell them!"

YOUR NEXT DAY: Who is it that the Spirit of Christ is prompting you to "Go and tell" today?

Day 7

NOTES about your Next Day

Day 8

"He is Risen"
Matthew 28:6

"He isn't here! He is risen from the dead, just as He said would happen. Come, see where His body was lying." Matthew 28:6 (NLT)

In 1920, during the beginnings of Soviet rule in Russia, a Communist propaganda leader named Nikoly Ivanovich Bukharin travelled from Moscow to Kiev to give a blistering "God is Dead" speech at an anti-God rally. For more than an hour, he ridiculed those who were followers of Christ. Once he completed his outrage, he asked the audience for questions but most in the audience were too intimated to speak. A Russian Orthodox priest slowly stepped to the platform, turned to the crowd, and proclaimed the Orthodox Easter greeting, "HE IS RISEN!" Immediately hundreds of people in the crowd jumped to their feet and shouted back, "HE IS RISEN INDEED!"

We too live in the NEXT DAY after the cross and resurrection. We know the outcome. As this world becomes more and more chaotic and sinister, we who are in Christ remain confident of our glorious future.

Dr. Herschel Hobbs was one of the great preachers of the last century and I had the privilege of serving as pastor in the same church in Mobile, Alabama. (He had been at our beloved Dauphin Way Baptist Church more than fifty years earlier than me, from 1945-1949). He wrote that during the time of Jesus there was a remarkable difference between those who didn't believe and those who believed:

"After the resurrection no enemy ever visited the tomb. Why? Fear. After Mary's proclamation "He is risen," there is no recorded visit by any disciples. Why? Faith and Knowledge." He was not there…He is risen. With that faith and knowledge of the reality of His resurrection, we have hope in a hopeless world."

YOUR NEXT DAY: We live in an increasing hostile culture to our faith in Jesus Christ. In light of His resurrection will you have the courage to stand and in His love refute the voices of disbelief with the simple statement: "He is Risen Indeed!"

Day 8

NOTES about your Next Day

Day 9

"Close Encounter"

Luke 24:33-34

And within the hour they were on their way back to Jerusalem. There they found the eleven disciples and the others who had gathered with them, who said, "The Lord has really risen! He appeared to Peter." Luke 24:33-34 (NLT)

Have you ever considered the difference between Judas and Peter? They were both disciples. They both pledged their love and loyalty to Jesus. And they both denied him. Yet Judas could not live with the guilt and hung himself. Peter was broken in his guilt. He had a close and secret encounter with Jesus following the resurrection and became the bold, godly disciple who would help shape Christianity for all of us. Ultimately, he too was put to death for his faith because he would not deny Christ.

I am sure that all who are reading this book have felt, at some time in life, they denied Christ by word, thought or deed. For those who are followers of Christ we can all identify with Peter. We have the "want to" but at times we lack the courage. In the most difficult times we often revert back to the old nature and before we know it our denial of Christ has been exposed by word or deed.

The news of the resurrection was great news indeed, but it must have caused conflict within Peter. The one Jesus had called the Rock must have felt his life crumbling into tiny stones. We can imagine the conversation he had with himself, "Do I run away or run to try and find Him? Will he forgive me? Should I follow the example of Judas and take my life?"

In the research for this book, I came across a few Scriptures that I had never fully explored, one in Luke 24:33-34 and the other in I Corinthians 15:3-5. Both remind us that Jesus had a close encounter of the Divine kind with Peter. It was the third appearance of Jesus following His resurrection. Peter and Jesus were alone in a secret meeting. We don't know what was said but we do know what happened. What Peter thought would be a tragic ending in his relationship turned out to be a new beginning.

YOUR NEXT DAY: Today is just between you and Lord. It is your own PRIVATE meeting with the resurrected Savior. What does He need to say to you? What do you need to say to Him? Remember, just as it was for Peter: sometimes our time of failure is the best time for Jesus to show us His way to success.

Day 9

NOTES about your Next Day

Day 10

"Next Witness Please"
I Corinthians 15:6-8

"After that, he was seen by more than 500 of his followers at one time, most of whom are still alive, though some have died. Then He was seen by James and later by all the apostles. Last of all, as though I had been born at the wrong time, I also saw him." (I Corinthians 15:6-8)

Through the years I have highly recommended Lee Strobel's book, *The Case for Christ*, to my friends who are honestly seeking truth in their search to confirm that Jesus is the Messiah. I love what this former investigative reporter wrote as he explained his own personal journey to ultimately come into a personal relationship with Jesus Christ.

"Without question, the amount of testimony and corroboration of Jesus' post-resurrection appearances is staggering. To put it into perspective, if you were to call each one of the witnesses to a court of law to be cross-examined for just fifteen minutes each, and you went around the clock Without question, the amount of testimony and corroboration of Jesus' post-resurrection appearances is staggering without a break, it would take you from breakfast on Monday until dinner on Friday to hear them all. After listening to 129 straight hours of eyewitness testimony, who could possibly walk away unconvinced?"

Two of those witnesses called would have told you that they were walking on the road to Emmaus, a small town about seven miles away from Jerusalem. A stranger walked with them along the way and they talked about everything that had happened the past three days. People who exercise (obviously this is not from my personal experience) tell me when you walk at a normal pace you can walk about three miles per hour. So they talked for over two hours, and yet did not realize they were walking with Jesus.

They did not recognize Him but they did recognize truth and once he sat down with them in the house He reclined at the table and broke the bread and gave it to them…THEN THEIR EYES WERE OPENED. These two witnesses went from being confused to convinced, from devastated to dynamic! The witnesses would later tell us in testimony "our hearts were ablaze when He was explaining scriptures to us while walking on the road!" We must remember the power of His spoken word and the witness of those who have met Him is how He continues to change lives today.

YOUR NEXT DAY: If you were called to the witness stand today to give

Day 10

NOTES about your Next Day

> These two witnesses went from being confused to convinced, from devastated to dynamic.

Day 11

"Locked Door? No Problem!"

John 20:19

That Sunday evening the disciples were meeting behind locked doors because they were afraid of the Jewish leaders. Suddenly, Jesus was standing there among them! "Peace be with you," He said. John 20:19 (NLT)

Locked doors can be a comfort or they can cause great consternation. It depends on whether you are locked in or locked out!

I had travelled into a little town called Burnsville in North Carolina to get some garden tools from Ace Hardware. (To be totally honest, I was picking the garden tools up for Cynthia as I had no intention of learning how to use them!) I was accompanied into town by Yogi, our Schipperke dog.

He loved the car and never missed a sight coming down the mountain into town. I pulled in and left Yogi in the unlocked car with the window open just an bit, knowing I'd only be in the store for a few minutes. I made my purchase and came back only to find that Yogi had jumped on door lock button and locked himself in the car. And my keys were laying in the seat.

Have you ever tried to explain to a dog how to jump over to the driver's seat and press the unlock button? Yogi looked perplexed as if to say, "Dude, I am burning up in this car, open the stupid door!" I looked back as if to say, "You dumb dog, you locked yourself in there!" Our problem was locked doors and he wasn't getting out and I wasn't getting in.

Two thousand years ago the disciples were still fearful for their lives after the horrible crucifixion of Jesus Christ. They had reassembled into the upper room, a familiar place and they "locked the doors!" Here is the huge difference between the disciples, me, Yogi and Jesus...locked doors are no problem for Jesus. Just as I was panicked, so were the disciples and Jesus CAME TO THEM. He took the initiative.

Locked doors were no problem for Jesus. He entered the house and set those free that saw and heard Him that day...and the world has never been the same. (By the way, it wasn't Jesus but it was a Burnsville policeman that opened the locked door and set Yogi free!)

YOUR NEXT DAY: What fears do you have locked away? What would happen if you would allow Jesus to unlock those fears and show you how you can overcome them through His life and love?

Day 11

NOTES about your Next Day

Day 12

"When the Church Really Becomes the Church"
Luke 24:49

"And now I will send the Holy Spirit, just as my Father promised. But stay here in the city until the Holy Spirit comes and fills you with power from heaven." Luke 24:49 (NLT)

The best average I could find of the number of Americans that are attending church today was 17.7 percent. That is down from nearly 40 percent in the 1980s. Everyone has a solution: "We need different worship styles," "We need multi-services and multiple campus locations," "We need to go back to what we used to do in the 80s," "We need to become more futuristic in order to reach this generation." Everyone has an answer and yet the decline continues in American churches.

During the forty days that Jesus was on this earth following His resurrection, He spoke about the "power" that would fill His people. We can read the first two chapters in the book of Acts to see how the power of God's Spirit came upon those first followers and we can see how God's power of His Spirit changed their lives and changed the early church. THEY (God's People) become witnesses to everyone around them. They no longer stayed hidden in a locked church by themselves waiting on the world to come to them…they went into the world.

Was it easy? No! The word *witness* means "martyr." History tells us that of the remaining 11 disciples, 10 of them were martyred for their boldness in proclaiming the truth about the Messiah.

The locked-up church was timid, frightened, and they preferred to just sit together in the comfort of their own little space and talk about Jesus…but nothing changed on the outside. Sounds a lot like the church in America doesn't it? So what's missing? I believe it is the yielding to the power of God's Spirit to once again fill us, embolden us to take the Gospel into a nation and a world that in in desperate need of truth. God has already given His Spirit to the Church. The early believers left the building long ago…so why are we still waiting?

YOUR NEXT DAY: Would you be willing to ask God's Spirit to fill your life today and give you the boldness to speak to your neighbors, friends, relatives, classmates or work associates about the power that has changed your life? They are desperately waiting for someone…it may as well be you.

Day 12

NOTES about your Next Day

Day 13

"Misperception"

John 20:24-25

"One of the disciples, Thomas (nicknamed the Twin), was not with the others when Jesus came. They told him, "We have seen the Lord!" But he replied, "I won't believe it unless I see the nail wounds in his hands, put my fingers into them, and place my hand into the wound in his side." John 20:24-25 (NLT)

History has had its share of misperceptions. Someone writes something from their perspective and others believe it as truth and before long the misperception becomes a reality. My whole life I heard how Napoleon was a short man. But he was actually the average height for a Frenchman. The confusion was a result of the difference in the French measurement of a foot and Imperial (British) measurement of a foot. He was 5-foot-2 in French measurement, but 5-foot-7 in the Imperial measurement we use. Personally, I'm going back to England and have them check me again.

"Doubting Thomas" should get a second look. For twenty centuries years we have given this label to this great disciple of our faith. One single act defined him for history. But is this fact or fiction? Let's clear up the misconception about Thomas:

• When Jesus told his disciples that they needed to go to Bethany, the other disciples balked. "The Jews tried to stone you and you want to go back there?" Thomas, as you remember, is the one also said, "Let's go so we may die with Him!"

• In John 14, Jesus tells the disciples that He is going to prepare a place for them and then said, "You know the way." It was Thomas that longed for truth, "We don't know where you're going, how can we know the way. Basically, he said, "I'm with you Jesus, just give me the address!"

• Finally, tradition tells us that Thomas is responsible for taking the gospel of Jesus Christ to India and there died a martyr in North India by the wounds of the four spears pierced into his body by the local soldiers.

Once Thomas saw the reality of the risen Savior, that was all the proof he needed. "You are my Lord and My God!"

YOUR NEXT DAY: In what area of your spiritual life are you struggling to make sense of your faith? Do you have the courage to seek Jesus, like Thomas, until your faith is secure? Ask Christ to strengthen your faith.

Day 13

NOTES about your Next Day

Day 14

"But Some Doubted....Seriously?"

Matthew 28:16-17

Then the eleven disciples left for Galilee, going to the mountain where Jesus had told them to go. When they saw Him, they worshiped Him—but some of them doubted. Matthew 28:16-17 (NLT)

The Risen Savior has already met with the disciples on two other occasions and this is the third. They are now waiting for Him in Galilee and He shows up, just as promised, and they worship Him. All logical up to this point.

Then we read...some of them doubted! I must admit this is a point of frustration for me. At least it was, until I stepped back and tried to look at this verse a different way.

Scripture says that some of the eleven doubted. But did they actually doubt Jesus? This was the third time they had seen the resurrected Savior. He already performed a miracle by walking through a locked door. They had already seen the nail prints in His hands and the scar from the spear in His side. Surely they would not have any doubts that Jesus was alive!

Here is my thought. Maybe it wasn't Jesus they were doubting. Maybe it was their own faith they doubted. "Do we have the courage and conviction to carry out His message to this world that is full of antagonistic people who are ready to kill us, just as they did our Savior? Is this the road I really want to walk?"

I know in my own life I have had those moments of doubt. I have never doubted Jesus, but I have often doubted if I had the absolute faith to trust and do exactly what He was asking of me.

If anything, the Resurrection of Jesus Christ should be all the evidence we need to follow Him in active obedience. Our doubts, and we all will have them, should be nothing more than a quick prayer asking the Lord to remind me that I cannot accomplish His work in my own power. He must prepare me and fill me for the assignment He has entrusted to me. And the same is true for you.

YOUR NEXT DAY: What is your greatest doubt today? Can you trace that back to a diminished faith? Tell God you trust Him and ask Him to give you the power to walk in obedience to the directions He gives to you.

Day 14

NOTES about your Next Day

> I have never doubted Jesus, but I have often doubted if I had the absolute faith to trust and do exactly what He was asking of me.

Day 15

"Catching Leadership"

John 21:3

Simon Peter said, "I'm going fishing." "We'll come too," they all said. So they went out in the boat, but they caught nothing all night. John 21:3 (NLT)

Have you ever noticed that the very traits that make a strong leader, if taken to their extreme, can set a leader up for failure? What may be viewed as a leader taking the initiative may turn out to be a flaw that leads to failure. Every leader has a leader and every leader must also be accountable to another leader. Such is the case with Simon Peter, the self-described leader of the disciples. In leadership, the result is a very thin line between successful leadership and failed leadership.

Jesus told the disciples to go the Sea of Galilee and wait for Him there. The Sea of Galilee is a very familiar place for the followers of Christ. Peter was especially familiar with this area as it was not only his home, but it also represented his old profession as a fisherman.

So the disciples are living in obedience, waiting at the Sea of Galilee when all of sudden the leader steps outside of obedience and says, "I'm going fishing" and the rest of the disciples play follow the leader.

The results of partial obedience: "So they went out in the boat, but they caught nothing all night."

Consider what happens when we live in partial obedience to the command of Christ: Our confidence becomes ego and ego begins to live in the false reality that everything is okay, even if I am not in full obedience to my Boss. Everyone loves a confident leader. Who isn't excited by the leader who walks into the room, commands attention, and takes control of the situation? But when a leader has an excess of confidence, it generally means ego takes over. Ego has a way of changing our plans, our visions, and our common sense and suddenly the conversation becomes all about the leader.

Thank God that failure is not permanent. However, there is a price to pay. On this particular day it was a fisherman's worst nightmare, taking a boat load of people out fishing and catching nada!

YOUR NEXT DAY: Can you identify one area of your life in which you are living in partial obedience? Reflect today how you can allow the Lord to turn your disappointment into victory in your life.

Day 15

NOTES about your Next Day

Day 16
"Remember!"

John 21:5-7

Jesus called out, "Fellows, have you caught any fish?" "No," they replied. Then He said, "Throw out your net on the right-hand side of the boat, and you'll get some!" So they did, and they couldn't haul in the net because there were so many fish in it. Then the disciple Jesus loved said to Peter, "It's the Lord!" When Simon Peter heard that it was the Lord, he put on his tunic (for he had stripped for work), jumped into the water, and headed to shore." John 21:5-7 (NLT)

Memory! What an amazing gift from God. Memories can be great tools to help us in our future, both good and bad memories. It's often said that a person is the sum of their memories. Your experience is what makes you who you are. It was memory that caused Peter to immediately identify the Lord and then not wait for the boat to row into shore but to jump in and get to Jesus as fast as possible.

All of us have experienced frustration in not being able to recall a fact from memory. It could be someone's name, or where we parked the car.

Some have suggested that memories decline, like fruit falling off a tree. But the research does not support this view. Instead, scientists have told us that our memory has a limitless capacity. Everything is stored in there but, without rehearsal of remembering, memories become harder to access.

Peter probably rehearsed this one memory over and over in his mind. It was just three years earlier, when Jesus asked two tired fishermen a key question: "Have you caught any fish." The question was not a jab at their ability, but a phrase that would ultimately lead them to obey the command, "Follow Me, and I will make you fishers of men." The Bible tells us at His word, "They left their nets and followed Him."

All of us have times in our life when we might think it would be easier to go back to the old way of life before we met the resurrected Savior. But our memories won't let us return to that which we know isn't God's best for us. The best memories are the ones He's yet to make with our lives.

YOUR NEXT DAY: What is your place of challenge today? It may be something that appears as innocent as going fishing, but if it is outside of God's will there is a good chance you'll end up empty and take others in the boat with you.

Day 16

NOTES about your Next Day

Day 17

"Fishing for People"
Matthew 4:18-20

One day as Jesus was walking along the shore of the Sea of Galilee, He saw two brothers—Simon, also called Peter, and Andrew—throwing a net into the water, for they fished for a living. Jesus called out to them, "Come, follow Me, and I will show you how to fish for people!" And they left their nets at once and followed Him. Matt. 4:18-20 (NLT)

Three years earlier before this Next Day, Jesus had already distinctly given the disciples their marching orders. Peter and Andrew were told, "I love the fact that you fish, but now I want you to fish for people!" I love it that Jesus used their profession to introduce them to their ministry.

Something similar happened to me.

I went to college on a scholarship in theatre. I had to have a scholarship as my family couldn't afford to send me to college. I never had any wild dreams that I would be some famous actor on stage or screen. I just didn't fit that mold and besides, I would have knocked Brad Pitt out of all those movies he has made!

However, it was a surprise when as a 20-year-old, God called me to become a minister. I was sitting by my girlfriend, who later became my wife (and continues to be my girlfriend). We both knew at once that we were about to experience something unexpected. God took the tools that He had given me in communication and creativity to use them for His glory.

Peter and Andrew knew they had prepared and practiced for years to understand everything they needed to know about fishing and now God would take that same preparation and use it by assigning them to carry out His plan.

YOUR NEXT DAY: God has prepared every one of us in His own way to be ready to carry out His call to reach this world with the message of hope, the message of eternal life that is possible only through Him. Think of how God has prepared and equipped you to fish for people and then ask the Lord to give you the names of the people you can reach through His power.

Day 17

NOTES about your Next Day

Day 18

"It's Not a Coincidence"
John 21:9

"When they got there, they found breakfast waiting for them—fish cooking over a charcoal fire, and some bread." John 21:9 (NLT)

I believe what we may view as a "coincidence" is instead truly a "divine appointment" that God has waiting for all of us.

Isn't it interesting that Jesus told His followers to wait at the Sea of Galilee and He would meet them there? Wait "at" the sea, not "on" the sea. God uses every situation in our life as one of those divine appointments that are intended to teach us and prepare us to be used for His glory.

When the disciples got off the boat after obeying the command of Jesus and "throwing their nets out on the other side," they came back with 153 fish. That's a big catch. But Jesus already had breakfast ready for them! He had the charcoal fire, perfectly prepared fish and indescribable bread.

WOW. Look at the lessons:

- Remember the feeding of the 5,000? Jesus reminds them He can meet their needs. Even though they had caught nothing all night, He has breakfast waiting for them in the morning. He supplies all our needs.
- Without Him, the fishing tournament would have been a disaster. But with Him...they blew everyone out of the water with a giant catch of 153 fish. "We can do all things through Christ who gives us strength!"
- The charcoal fire? Another reminder that just a week ago Peter had been sitting by a charcoal fire in the courtyard of Caiaphas when he started cursing in his denial of the Savior. Now the fire reminds him that Jesus will give Peter the opportunity to repent and be restored. Once forgiven, Jesus ultimately tells Peter, "Go and feed my sheep!"

A coincidence? More like a well-designed, well-timed reminder that God had a plan all along.

YOUR NEXT DAY: Looking back over this past week can you identify a "divine appointment" God provided for you? How did that impact you? What does God want you to take from that fresh encounter?

Day 18

NOTES about your Next Day

Day 19

"Don't Give Up on Your Family"
I Corinthians 15:7

I was an associate pastor in Oklahoma City and one Sunday Danny, a young father hooked on drugs, made yet another trip to the altar to confess his stronghold and swear it would never happen again. His godly wife came with him…again…and said, "I know Jesus can heal Him, I know he can change." I hate to admit this, but I agreed with what she said intellectually and spiritually but I really just couldn't see it happening. This was at least the fourth time he had "turned it over to the Lord" and yet he was right back at the altar again.

James was the half-brother of Jesus and basically he thought his brother was a religious nut who had lost his mind. Mark 3:21 says, "When His family heard what was happening, they tried to take Him away" and "He's out of His mind." John 7:5 says, "For even His brothers didn't believe in Him."

I often wonder how many of us have written off our family members and think in our hearts, "They will never change!" Probably far too many of us. But Jesus never gave up on His family. As a matter of record, Jesus sought out his brother after the resurrection: *"Then He was seen by James and later by all the apostles."* (1 Corinthians 15:7)

James became a great man of God. As the leader of the church in Jerusalem, he was ultimately stoned to death as a martyr. I am so thankful his brother, the Savior of the World, didn't give up on him.

By the way, years later I was pastoring in Florida and received a Christmas card from Danny with a picture of his wife and children. He had become a minister, completed his education and was pastoring in a small town in Oklahoma. He wrote to say thanks. But honestly, thanks goes to the Lord and to his wife, who never gave up!

YOUR NEXT DAY: Who in your family needs to know Jesus or is away from Him in their spiritual walk? Consider taking them to lunch or spending an afternoon with them to see where they are spiritually and talk about ways you can take steps forward together.

Day 19

NOTES about your Next Day

Day 20

"Refresher Course"
Luke 24:44-47

Then He said, "When I was with you before, I told you that everything written about Me in the law of Moses and the prophets and in the Psalms must be fulfilled." Then He opened their minds to understand the Scriptures. And He said, "Yes, it was written long ago that the Messiah would suffer and die and rise from the dead on the third day. It was also written that this message would be proclaimed in the authority of His name to all the nations, beginning in Jerusalem: 'There is forgiveness of sins for all who repent.'" Luke 24:44-47 (NLT)

In Luke 24:44, the Messiah is providing His disciples with a refresher course regarding the resurrection. Jesus is reminding the disciples to take a look back to take a look forward. He is reminding them about some of the writings that He taught them before going to the cross.

It is interesting that He directed their attention to the Old Testament with the following descriptions: The Law of Moses, the Prophets, and the Psalms. Jesus was showing how the Old Testament provided all the support you need to point people to the fact that He is the Promised Messiah.

I love using the Old Testament to show the truth of the New Testament. I enjoy teaching out of the Old Testament because of the opportunity to paint the picture of Jesus through the eyes of the Old Testament writers.

There are three themes that are repeated over and over again in the Old Testament. The Old Testament calls on us to…
     1. Repent
     2. Remember
     3. Rekindle

It's not by accident that the Savior would take the time after the resurrection to open our minds and hearts to the glorious truth revealed in the Old Testament. Behold, the old has become new!

YOUR NEXT DAY: Jesus never said or did anything by accident. The fact that He took the time following His resurrection to "tie the old to the new" is a reminder of our responsibility to follow His example. Using the Old Testament to reveal Christ is a tremendous way to encourage our Jewish friends to "dig a little deeper" in the Old Testament. Today, pray for one of your Jewish friends, that you might love them and share with them Christ revealed using just the Old Testament.

Day 20

NOTES about your Next Day

> Jesus is reminding the disciples to take a look back to take a look forward.

Day 21

"It's Friday, but Sunday's Comin'!"

I Corinthians 5:14

I never tire of hearing Tony Campolo preach the sermon entitled, "It's Friday, but Sunday's Comin." The magnificent sermon was first delivered by African American preacher S. M. Lockridge. No matter how terrible things look in life, they're going to get better. After all, everyone has a "Good Friday" that is anything but good. Regardless of your circumstances, *the events of the following Sunday changed everything.*

While the sermon is a masterpiece, it is the message that is crucial to hear. The resurrection of Jesus Christ demonstrates to me that no matter how bad things might look in this present moment, God has the power to change not only me but He also has the resurrection power to change my circumstances. God remains in control and as I look to him, I can be assured that He will arrange the outcome according to his plan.

I can't tell you the number of times over 40 years of ministry that God has taken my Friday of despair and brought victory out of what appeared to be certain disaster. Proverbs 21:21 says the believer "who pursues righteousness and love finds life, prosperity and honor."

I was in the hospital with a friend of mine, and his elderly mom had been in a coma for almost ten days. Her husband, who had been a pastor his entire life preceded her in death. Now I was standing with my friend by his mom's bedside. He asked me, "Pastor, would you pray that Jesus will come and take her home?" We held hands with his precious mom, prayed a simple prayer asking for Christ to take her home then said "Amen."

Suddenly, this woman who had not spoken for days opened her eyes wide and said, "He's here!" She closed her eyes and passed away. James and I looked at each other and then he said, "WOW, the power of the resurrection was just on display for us to witness!"

Yes, it may be Friday for many of you who are reading today's devotional, but Sunday's coming!

YOUR NEXT DAY: In what area of your life do you need the demonstration of the resurrection power of Jesus? I can assure you, His resurrection is NOT smoke and mirrors but is the power of the Messiah available to you today.

Day 21

NOTES about your Next Day

Day 22

"You Don't Know How Bad I've Been"
1 Corinthians 15:21-22

So you see, just as death came into the world through a man, now the resurrection from the dead has begun through another man. Just as everyone dies because we all belong to Adam, everyone who belongs to Christ will be given new life. 1 Corinthians 15:21-22 (NLT)

Tommy was a detective with the police department in Mobile, Alabama. He is a very godly man, loved the Lord and sought to make Christ known. I will never forget the day he called me and asked to meet him at the jail. They had tracked down a man who 40 years earlier had beaten three young African American boys and then hung them from a tree.

Although the incident had been in the news for four decades, no one had hope that the cold case would be solved. From a tip in the state of Ohio, the man was discovered living in a nursing home, near death. He was extradited to Mobile and charged with the murders.

I met Tommy at the jail and they arranged for me to talk to the man who was charged with the crime. I was torn. I couldn't imagine how someone could do this and I wasn't sure what good it would do for me to speak with him. As I walked into the holding area I saw an elderly, very sick man sitting across from me behind a table.

It was difficult to picture this man as the monster he had been. I introduced myself and he immediately said, "I did it and I'm going to go to hell!" I paused and responded, "Yes sir, you are going to go to hell unless you ask Jesus to forgive you and become your Savior." After an hour of explaining the Gospel, the man prayed with me to give his life to Christ.

The man who was not fit to live on this earth died before the trial. I'm sure he was surprised to be welcomed by another man who was hung on a tree two thousand years ago. The old life was gone and behold, all had become new by the miracle of the Messiah.

YOUR NEXT DAY: Is there anyone in your life that you feel has committed such a grievous offense that they could never spend eternity in Heaven with Christ? Place their name in your journal and remember this man who said, "You don't know how bad I've been." Remember, God saved him and forgave him just like He did me.

Day 22

NOTES about your Next Day

Day 23

"The Dark Side of the Soul"

John 20:19

A friend of mine named Peter Lord adapted a 16th-century term to describe "the dark side of the soul." Peter said there will be times in your life when your experiences tell you that God is absent, or even dead. In those times, you must not trust your experience but you must trust His truth. The man or woman who comes through the "dark side of the soul" will survive even more assured of the resurrection power of Jesus Christ.

That Sunday evening the disciples were meeting behind locked doors because they were afraid of the Jewish leaders. Suddenly, Jesus was standing there among them! "Peace be with you," he said. John 20:19 (NLT)

The disciples' expectations of living and learning from Jesus changed in their experience of His death. Their experience was definitely a dark side of the soul. This "dark side" told them that God was absent, that He had no power and was inactive during Jesus' crucifixion. The disciples were absolutely terrified and they ran in all different directions as he was beaten and crucified. Now they were hiding behind locked doors praying the Jewish leaders wouldn't discover their hiding place.

But even the darkest side of the soul has an bright awakening if you are a follower of Christ. For the believer, this dark side does not last forever. In the very midst of the disciples' terror, the resurrected Christ appears and proves that trusting their experience rather His word was wrong. God had been present and active all along. That's good for us to remember when our own souls take a turn in darkness. It is His resurrection that assures us we walk by faith, not by feeling.

YOUR NEXT DAY: Can you name a time in your life when you trusted in your experience rather than the truth you know as a follower of Christ? What did you do to move beyond your feelings and move into your faith walk and victory?

Day 23

NOTES about your Next Day

Day 24
"For 40 Days..."
Acts 1:1-3

In my first book I told you, Theophilus, about everything Jesus began to do and teach until the day He was taken up to heaven after giving His chosen apostles further instructions through the Holy Spirit. During the forty days after His crucifixion, He appeared to the apostles from time to time, and He proved to them in many ways that He was actually alive. And He talked to them about the Kingdom of God. Acts 1:1-3 (NLT)

Forty days following His Easter resurrection, Jesus showed the world death could not conquer Him. The religious leaders called the Messiah a blasphemer, but the 40 days Jesus spent in Jerusalem and nearby areas has met little challenge. The Jewish historian Josephus referred to the resurrection, as did other early writers:

We can look two generations after the resurrection and Eusebius interviewed several people who had known people who saw the resurrected Messiah during these 40 days. He reports that people told him of miracles, and even cited letters written about seeing the risen Jesus.

In other words, some people might not have joined the Christ-followers, although believers multiplied rapidly, even in the face of persecution. However, very few people disputed His resurrection.

The number 40 appears 146 times in the Bible, a number that obviously has biblical significance. We think of the years God's people spent in the desert, or the days Jesus spent in the wilderness being tempted by Satan following his baptism, or the days Moses was on Mount Moriah, or the time Jonah was in Nineveh. And, of course, the number of days between the Resurrection and the Ascension of the Messiah. Theologians tell us that the number 40 signifies a time of testing, trials, probation, or a time of provision and prosperity. Obviously, the last definition comes closest to the resurrected Christ before He ascended. They certainly were active days.

YOUR NEXT DAY: The last verse of the last gospel's last book, the book of John tells us, "Jesus also did many other things. If they were all written down, I suppose the whole world could not contain the books that would be written." John 21:25 (NLT) Think about this verse. Only a small part of the actions of Jesus while on earth have actually been written down. As you think about how your next days after Easter are transformed by the Word of God, highlight the most important verses that come to your heart.

Day 24

NOTES about your Next Day

Testimonium Flavianum
Written by Roman historian Flavius Josephus at the end of the first century

"About this time there lived Jesus, a wise man if indeed one ought to call him a man. For he was one who wrought surprising feats and was a teacher of such people as accept the truth gladly. He won over many Jews and many of the Greeks. He was the Christ. When Pilate, upon hearing him accused by men of the highest standing amongst us, had condemned him to be crucified, those who had in the first place come to love him did not give up their affection for him. On the third day he appeared to them restored to life, for the prophets of God had prophesied these and countless other marvelous things about him. And the tribe of the Christians, so called after him, has still to this day not disappeared."

Day 25

"It's About A Relationship...Not Your Religion"

Acts 8::1-3

For my entire ministry I have told everyone I speak to, when we are talking about faith in Jesus Christ, "It's not about your religion, it's about your relationship to Jesus Christ!"

I am firmly convinced that religion has done more damage in the history of this world than any other single factor. Religion originates with man but a personal relationship with God originates with Jesus. Saul, who would later be called Paul after his conversion, knew about Jesus. He knew about the "new religion" and knew the multitudes that were following Jesus.

No doubt he was fueled with hatred by religious leaders he respected and when he witnessed the murder of Stephen it lit a fire in his soul to do everything within his power to destroy the spread of Christianity. After all, he was doing this in the name of his religion! Read the verse that triggered his anger and hatred toward Christians....

Saul was one of the witnesses, and he agreed completely with the killing of Stephen. A great wave of persecution began that day, sweeping over the church in Jerusalem and all the believers except the apostles were scattered through the regions of Judea and Samaria. (Some devout men came and buried Stephen with great mourning.) But Saul was going everywhere to destroy the church. He went from house to house, dragging out both men and women to throw them into prison. Acts 8:1-3 (NLT)

Even as I write this, I cannot escape the image in my mind of 21 godly Coptic Christians who were beheaded for their faith. With audio playing while the world watched, the Christians one by one beheaded. The last thing we heard them say in their Egyptian language was "Blessed be the Name of the Lord...Bless you, Jesus!"

Our prayer is simple. Jesus Christ miraculously met Saul face to face while he was travelling to persecute more Christians. After that encounter, Saul became Paul. It wasn't just a name change, it was a life change...an eternal life change.

YOUR NEXT DAY: How can you pray today for those enemies of the Lord Jesus Christ? Pray that God would show them that religion kills and destroys, but a relationship with God through Christ brings hope, love and the promise of eternal life.

Day 25

NOTES about your Next Day

Day 26

"Doubt Defined"

I Corinthians 15:12-15

But tell me this—since we preach that Christ rose from the dead, why are some of you saying there will be no resurrection of the dead? For if there is no resurrection of the dead, then Christ has not been raised either. And if Christ has not been raised, then all our preaching is useless, and your faith is useless. And we apostles would all be lying about God—for we have said that God raised Christ from the grave. But that can't be true if there is no resurrection of the dead.
1 Corinthians 15:12-15 (NLT)

Webster Dictionary defines doubt as "the uncertainty of belief or opinion that often interferes with decision-making."

Obviously, the resurrection was the centerpiece of the Apostle's teaching as they had been instructed by Jesus during the 40-day period between His resurrection and His ascension. Yet in spite of the eyewitness reports, there were still those who doubted....even some of those who were IN THE CHURCH that doubted the resurrection of Jesus Christ.

Here is the problem that Paul had with the Christians at Corinth and the problem that I have with the same type of teaching that originated two thousand years ago…it is a teaching that suggests Christianity can exist without the Resurrection.

Paul reminded all of us that if that were the case then…
- Our preaching is useless, our faith has no foundation and we are false witness
- We are still responsible for our sins, which means eternal separation from God.
- Those loved ones who have died have no hope.
- We are a mess spiritually and shouldn't waste more time with our faith!

Even though we continue to preach and teach the resurrection of Jesus Christ we still come face to face with the same results as the Apostle Paul did two thousand years ago. "When they heard Paul speak about the resurrection of the dead, some laughed in contempt, but others said, 'We want to hear more about this later.'" Acts 17:32 (NLT)

YOUR NEXT DAY: Doubts are normal in the Christian life. However, there are honest doubters who search for ultimate proof and there are unfortunate individuals who are proud of their doubts! Write down the doubts you have today in your spiritual walk and ask the Lord to give you the evidence that brings His peace to your life.

Day 26

NOTES about your Next Day

Day 27
"Which Thief are You?"
Luke 23:39-43

When Jesus was walking with His disciples after the resurrection, one of the first beneficiaries of His resurrection was already walking in heaven. The thief beside Jesus on the cross put His hope in the Savior and was one of the first to experience true life. How different the story must have seemed from the other side. Yet how tragic it also must have been for the thief on the other cross who chose not to walk in the way of God's forgiveness when he had the chance.

I'm sure you remember the story:

"One of the criminals hanging beside him scoffed, "So you're the Messiah, are you? Prove it by saving yourself—and us, too, while you're at it!" But the other criminal protested, "Don't you fear God even when you have been sentenced to die? We deserve to die for our crimes, but this man hasn't done anything wrong." Then he said, "Jesus, remember me when you come into your Kingdom." And Jesus replied, "I assure you, today you will be with me in paradise."
Luke 23:39-43 (NLT)

Have you ever struggled with the concept of forgiveness? I know I have. There are times that I have felt very much like one of the thieves. "We deserve what we are getting…" Perhaps it is difficult to comprehend that Jesus can forgive us because it is so hard for us to forgive the people who have wronged us.

I can't even imagine what must have gone through the mind of the thief who was forgiven by Jesus on the cross while He was dying. I try to close my eyes and put myself in his position and hear the words escape the Savior's lips, "Today you shall be with me in Paradise."

I wonder if before Jesus started His 40-day reunion tour following the resurrection, He made a quick stop in glory to introduce His new Friend to the Father: "Today, you shall be with me in Paradise."

YOUR NEXT DAY: Consider these questions: Is there anyone in your life that you have not forgiven? If so, then how can you reconcile that relationship? Who do you know in your circle that if they were to die today they would most likely not be in paradise with Jesus? Connect with them, share your story and encourage them to explore the claims of Christ.

Day 27

NOTES about your Next Day

Day 28
"The Big Elephant in the Room"
I Corinthians 15:6

The Bible tells us that after the resurrection of Jesus Christ that He spent the next 40 days on this earth, visiting with the disciples, talking to friends and on one occasion meeting more than 500 people. The one question that we need to ask in our 40-day journey is what they call an "elephant in the room." Everyone knows something has happened, but no one is acknowledging the fact.

WHY DID JESUS STAY ON THIS EARTH FOR 40 DAYS FOLLOWING THE RESURRECTION?

The obvious reason is that Jesus wanted to demonstrate to His followers that He truly had conquered death and He is alive.

His followers knew the Roman authorities had put Jesus to death. They had watched them take Him from the cross and place Him in the guarded tomb. They were filled with fear and went into hiding. Now their hopes were shattered. They had forgotten His promise that He would return from the grave. They had no future.

But Jesus was resurrected, and more than that, walked among these same followers. The greatest miracle in all history had just taken place: Jesus Christ is alive! It was during those 40 days that Christ appeared to not only His disciples but to many other groups of people. Twenty years later Paul reminded us: "He appeared to more than five hundred of the brothers at the same time, most of whom are still living" (1 Corinthians 15:6).

Jesus used the 40 days to teach His disciples and prepare them for the task of telling the world about the Messiah and His amazing gift of forgiveness and eternal life.

YOUR NEXT DAY: How are you using the time God has given you on this earth to make a difference in someone's eternity? Jesus used the 40 days wisely and maximized His time preparing others for eternity. Take some time today in your journal and consider how you will use your time this week. What portion of that time is set apart to tell others about your faith and His story?

Day 28

NOTES about your Next Day

> Why did Jesus stay around for 40 days following His resurrection?

Day 29
"An Appointment with Death"
Hebrews 9:27

The resurrection is not something that just happened two thousand years ago. The resurrection changed the way we look at life today. It changed the way we look at death. It has changed the way we look at our future.

Jimmy worked at the Texaco in the community where I pastored my first church in Hobart, Oklahoma. He worked all through the summer getting ready to start college. The owner of the gas station loved the Lord and asked me if I would speak with Jimmy about his faith. Every time I filled up my car, I would talk to Jimmy about visiting our church and he would say the same thing every time, "One of these days I'm going to surprise you, Preacher!"

The last time I spoke with Jimmy I felt led of the Lord not just to invite him to church, but to invite him to trust Jesus as His personal Savior. However, the answer was still the same, "One of these days I'm going to surprise you, Preacher."

His words were prophetic. He did surprise me and the entire community when that same day he went to the lake with a friend and drowned. His family asked me to preach his funeral and I used the topic, "An Appointment with Death" based on this passage in Hebrews 9:27, *"And just as each person is destined to die once and after that comes judgment."*

The greatest threat we face in the future is death. The fear of death controls us much more than we realize. However, the resurrection of Jesus Christ takes the surprise out of death for those who have trusted Him as their Savior. His resurrection, and the 40 days He spent on earth teaching and showing people the reality that He had conquered death, gave hope to everyone! In Christ there is life beyond the grave. Death is no longer to be a surprise, that unknown danger ... it is now a door by which we enter eternity with Him.

At the time of death for a follower of Christ, our future is certain and there will be NO SURPRISES for the child of God." We all have an appointment with death...It would be a tragedy if you are surprised.

YOUR NEXT DAY: Ask yourself this question: "Will I be surprised at where I spend eternity?" If your response is yes, then it's time to review what Jesus said during the 40 days following His resurrection. Trust Him as Your Savior.

Day 29

NOTES about your Next Day

Day 30
"You Can't Fool All the People All the Time"
I Corinthians 15:6

"After that, he was seen by more than 500 of his followers at one time, most of whom are still alive, though some have died." I Corinthians 15:6 (NLT)

P.T. Barnum said, "You can fool all of the people some of the time. And you can fool some of the people all of the time. But you cannot fool all of the people all of the time."

I believe there was a reason that Jesus was intentional about being seen here on earth prior to His ascension by more than 500 at once. If you have one or two people who say, "We saw Him alive after the crucifixion" then you have the opportunity to call out the conspiracy theorists. But here is Christ in the midst of "more than 500" people. You might as well have the "Christ the Redeemer" statue located in Rio de Janeiro that is 98 feet tall and 12 feet wide. In other words…YOU CAN'T MISS SEEING HIM!

I believe that Jesus chose to be seen by the masses as well as by the few because the testimony of His power over death would be dependent upon the truthful testimony of those who actually came face to face with the Messiah. Think about it for a moment. Can you imagine the 500 running home that evening telling their own story of having just seen the Risen Savior?

We have seen Him by faith and today millions of Christians are called to follow the example of the 500 and run and tell someone, anyone…but please tell someone.

The average attendance of the church in America has dropped from 40 percent to less than 17 percent in the past 40 years. Perhaps what we need is the same type of awakening that took place when suddenly, totally unexpected, the Risen Savior walked into the lives of more than 500 people. Something happened that day, and this world has never been the same.

YOUR NEXT DAY: One thing to remember today is that it would have been easy to say, "Well someone else saw Him so I don't need to say anything." How tragic that would be. I often say that our relationship with Jesus Christ is personal, but it is never private. Take the time today to write one letter to a friend and share what Christ has done for you this week.

Day 30

NOTES about your Next Day

Day 31

"Beyond Reasonable Doubt"

Acts 1:1-3

I love television shows about lawyers, especially the cross-examination. The defendant's attorney will try to create "reasonable doubt." But it doesn't matter how good the lawyer is, proof is proof!

"In my first book I told you, Theophilus, about everything Jesus began to do and teach until the day he was taken up to heaven after giving his chosen apostles further instructions through the Holy Spirit. **During the forty days after His crucifixion, He appeared to the apostles from time to time, and He proved to them in many ways that He was actually alive.** *And He talked to them about the Kingdom of God."* Acts 1:1-3 (NLT)

The phrase "He proved to them in many ways" has the essence of "infallible proofs." Luke makes sure to use the plural form of the phrase indicating that Jesus proved His resurrection to them over and over again.

The disciples had seen for themselves the trauma of Jesus' own trial. They had seen Him give proof during His life of all that He claimed. Then they saw Him taken to an unfair cross to serve an undeserved sentence. They had seen His lifeless body taken from that cross and they had seen Him placed in a borrowed tomb. There may not have been much the disciples could trust themselves to know during those dark days, but they knew this one thing: Jesus was definitely dead.

There was only ONE WAY TO remove any reasonable doubt! Jesus had been dead. Yet now He stood before them, very much alive, giving proof after proof that He had overcome both death and doubt. So Jesus reached out to them and gave them hope they could hold on to: "Look at my hands. Look at my feet. You can see that it's really me. Touch me and make sure that I am not a ghost, because ghosts don't have bodies, as you see that I do." Luke 24:39 (NLT)

Like the world's greatest attorney, Jesus made sure we could celebrate these 40 days after Easter "beyond any reasonable doubt."

YOUR NEXT DAY: Take some time to think about the different ways Jesus appeared to His followers so that He could remove any reasonable doubt. What senses did He use to demonstrate His presence? What words did He use to communicate that He was really there?

Day 31

NOTES about your Next Day

Day 32

"All I Know About Superheroes, I Learned from My Grandson, Strong"

Acts 1:1-8

I am blessed to have a six-year old grandson that is a superhero. He started as Peter Pan then became Batman and quickly moved to Superman. But was disappointed with his attempts at flying and so now is someone new called SONIC….all I know about Sonic is that he is blue and superfast. Looks more like a fast Smurf than a superhero but…then again what do I know about superheroes? All I know is that Strong is doing the very best he can to recruit, Truman, his one year-old brother into the order of the super secret Superhero club. It's all about POWER!

We dreamed about power when we were kids and many people never grow out of their love for power…but few really understand REAL POWER!

Right before Jesus ascended to Heaven He spoke this amazing promise to His followers:

"But you will receive power when the Holy Spirit comes upon you. And you will be my witnesses, telling people about me everywhere— in Jerusalem, throughout Judea, in Samaria, and to the ends of the earth."

Think for a moment where you need POWER. Jesus told all of us who are His followers that our power should be focused on one thing: telling people about the power of the cross that can change the eternal destiny of those we know and love.

YOUR NEXT DAY: If you are an individual who does not already have a personal relationship with the Risen Savior, then God will give you His power. Pray today for His power:
- to forgive you
- to cleanse you of your sin
- to fill your life with His presence.

If you have trusted Christ, then list the names of five family members or friends who need to receive Christ and then pray that God will give you the POWER to be His witness to those you love. Go ahead, try on that superhero costume…you will be surprised that it is a perfect fit.

Day 32

NOTES about your Next Day

> My grandson started as Peter Pan then became Batman and quickly moved to Superman. But he was disappointed with his attempts at flying.

Day 33

"Name the State Where Jerusalem is the Capital"

Acts 1:1-8

Little did we know that one of the last things Jesus told us on this earth was that He wanted to give us a geography lesson. Look again at Acts 1:8:

But you will receive power when the Holy Spirit comes upon you. And you will be my witnesses, telling people about me everywhere—in Jerusalem, throughout Judea, in Samaria, and to the ends of the earth. Acts 1:8

Quick quiz! Tell me the name of the state where Jerusalem was the capital? Using the context of His own geographical reality, Jesus says our witness should begin at home, move to our city, move then to our state and then move to our nation and then to the uttermost part of the world.

How are we doing with this challenge? I'm afraid we not doing a very good job with our responsibility. I'm not sure if it is we don't know our geography or we don't know our Savior.

More than 91 percent of our resources—buildings, money, leaders—are spent in countries where there's an overwhelming Christian majority. But in nations where fewer than half of the people know Jesus, we spend just 3 percent of our resources. For every dollar we spend to reach people who are already Christians, we spend less than 3 cents on reaching those who most desparately need to know the Lord. However, Christians worldwide spend around $8 BILLION dollars PER YEAR going to the more than 500 conferences just to TALK about missions. Crazy.

My precious wife Cynthia, along with my long-term partner in ministry Mike Jeffries, have always had a heart for the geography of grace. There are many, many others who share their passion but still not enough. Our world today is in crisis and Christians in many nations are losing their lives simply because they Follow the Leader.

YOUR NEXT DAY: A great exercise for your Next Day journey would be to pray for the missionaries who are in foreign nations today and ask God for their protection. Secondly, pray that we will give our resources and our personal lives to take that message of truth to the entire world. It is great to have the knowledge of geography, but it is a far greater value for you to actually make a difference in those nations without Christ.

Day 33

NOTES about your Next Day

Day 34

"You Gotta Start at Home"
Acts 1:7-8

But you will receive power when the Holy Spirit comes upon you. And you will be my witnesses, telling people about me everywhere—in Jerusalem, throughout Judea, in Samaria, and to the ends of the earth." Acts 1:7-8 (NLT)

Last words are important. Especially if they're spoken by someone you love and care about. Jesus had some last words, too, but they weren't the last words at His death. Jesus intentionally shared with His followers these last words He would speak on earth, precisely because these are the words that lead to life.

Jesus is not unclear about these words. He doesn't give us a mystery we have to figure out. His words aren't a riddle to be solved. They're not an enigma that needs interpretation. No, He's very clear and He tells all of us who are followers, "you will receive power when the Holy Spirit comes upon you. And you will be my witnesses, telling people about Me everywhere…"

The disciples have their marching orders and they are to start in the town in which they live. At this time in history, the disciples were in Jerusalem and so Jesus said, "START HERE!"

Where is "HERE" for you?
    What city do you live in: _____
Let's make this a little more personal.
    *What street do you live on*_____.
Finally, let's really get serious about this command.
    What are the names of your neighbors who
    do not have a relationship with Jesus?
_____
_____

YOUR NEXT DAY: If you have trusted Christ, you have the power of His Spirit in you. Now all you have to do is obey. Your job: Tell your neighbors about Jesus. Tell them through your actions but also through your words. Invite them to join you for worship and then take them out for lunch after church. Eighty percent of all new church members say they first visited the church because a friend asked them to visit. Write in your journal the names of the people you will pray for and then invite to join you for worship in your church.

.

Day 34

NOTES about your Next Day

> Jesus is not unclear about these words. He doesn't give us a mystery we have to figure out. His words aren't a riddle to be solved.

Day 35

"Can You Name Your State Bird?"

Acts 1:8

"But you will receive power when the Holy Spirit comes upon you. And you will be my witnesses, telling people about me everywhere—in Jerusalem, throughout JUDEA, in Samaria, and to the ends of the earth." Acts 1:8 (NLT)

If you were to ask me, "What is the state bird of Florida," I would tell you I don't know. (I did look it up and it's the mockingbird.) One fact I know about our state that we have called home for 25 years is that we have people that love to honk their car horn if you don't immediately…I mean IMMEDIATELY drive as soon as the light is green. I refer to them by many names…some would not be appropriate for a devotional book so let's just call them "The Honk-A-Second" drivers. WHY? Because if you don't take off within one second when the light turns green then you are a prime candidate to receive "a FLORIDA honk and a partial hand wave that resembles a bird (and not the state bird)."

In truth, I love Florida. I love South Florida. I love the diversity in our city and the fact that our church reflects the diversity of where we live. We are a multi-racial and multi-cultural church and I honestly LOVE IT.

Maybe I love our church more than I love the people in our state. It's no secret that we are one of the top ten unchurched states in America.

When Jesus told His followers to go into their state, Judea, they knew that their state was hostile to the Gospel. Judea was the toughest place for Christians and believers there suffered some of the greatest persecution. While our modern-day persecution cannot compare, I believe that our state and every state will be hostile to our creed until we move outside the security of our church walls and begin to show the people what Jesus really looks like. Sadly, now less than 10 percent of the citizens of Florida go to church.

We may not know the name of our state bird but it is even more tragic that the people of our state don't know the Name of our Savior!

YOUR NEXT DAY: Pray for your state today. Prayerfully consider one action step that you could take to help make Christ known in the places closest to where you live.

Day 35

NOTES about your Next Day

Day 36

"You Shall be My Witnesses in Jerusalem.... or, is it Fort Lauderdale?"

Acts 1:1-8

Name the city in which you live... ours is Fort Lauderdale but I hope that readers from many cities will be reading this book. Jesus was talking to the disciples about the city in which they lived and He commanded, "YOU SHALL BE MY WITNESSES..."

I have noticed that in my 40 years of ministry it is much easier for Christians to go to a foreign land to be witnesses for Christ. People get all excited to see the children and families trust Christ in Nicaragua on our mission site but ask those same people to go next door and be His witness to your neighbors...well, that's usually just not going to happen as easily.

My question is simple, yet convicting. "How can we raise money to go on a mission tour, take pictures of families that are in desperate need of the love of Christ, but not go next door and share that same passion. WHY!"

(In fact, it's much more likely that the only way you'll go to your neighbor is to go out of the country first....kind of like on-the-job training. There's something about being out of your own context—in another country—that gives you courage. But you have to take that courage and bring it back to America and to your own street!)

The church in America is in rapid decline. Something is drastically wrong. Jesus said "Start in your city making me known...then move out into all the world." In 1980, 40 percent of Americans went to church...today, the number is less than 17 percent. And in South Florida, 93 percent of our residents do not attend anyone's church.

There has never been a more crucial hour. God's people must revisit Acts 1:8...we must capture the intent of His last words on this earth. If you can't walk next door and share the love of Jesus Christ with those closest to you, then why travel to Africa or South America. I believe we will be held accountable for this call: to our city, to our country, to our world.

YOUR NEXT DAY: Take a moment and pray for three neighbors who may not KNOW the Risen Christ of Easter on a personal basis. Write down their names and then pray and look for the opportunity to fulfill this last command of Christ before He ascended to Heaven.

Day 36

NOTES about your Next Day

Day 37

"To the Ends of the Earth"
Acts 1:8

"But you will receive power when the Holy Spirit comes upon you. And you will be my witnesses, telling people about me everywhere—in Jerusalem, throughout Judea, in Samaria, and to the ends of the earth." Acts 1:8 (NLT)

The last words that Jesus spoke on this earth were geared toward reaching the nations with the Gospel. God has always had a heart and purpose that His name and fame be lifted up among every tribe and tongue and people and nation. There are 6.6 billion people and 3.3 billion people have not yet had enough access to the Gospel that they need so they might believe. This number is incomprehensible.

Think about this number for a moment. There are 11,120 different people groups in our world today. More than half, seven thousand of them, have less than two percent who believe in Jesus. More than 3,500 of those people groups do not have ONE SINGLE PERSON who has professed faith in Christ.

If we are to make Jesus known in this world then we need to pray that God would call and send workers into the world to reach these different people groups...especially these roups that do not have ONE SINGLE CHRISTIAN among their population.

YOUR NEXT DAY: For today's response to your journal take a moment and think about what you can do to better prepare yourself to pray and reach those who do not know Christ today? I have an idea. I will provide you with some suggestions and then you choose a couple of them to help better understand people groups who do not have acces to the Gospel.

_____Read a book to understand their culture
_____Access online resources explaining these groups
_____Learn about their religion
_____Identify if you speak the language of one of these people groups
_____Send financial support to our missions ministry
_____Pick one people group and start to pray for them for a year

Day 37

NOTES about your Next Day

www.PeopleGroups.org

When you walk through an average day in the United States or Europe, you might think that everyone everywhere has access to the Good News of Jesus. Even if everyone doesn't believe, at least they know something about Him.

But there are seven thousand people groups around the world who have little or no access to who Jesus is or what He did for them.

To find out more about these unreached, unengaged and even uncontacted people around the world, access the International Mission Board site **www.PeopleGroups.org**.

Day 38

"I Can Do Anything I Want to Do"
Matthew 28:18-20

Jesus came and told His disciples, "I have been given all authority in heaven and on earth. Therefore, go and make disciples of all the nations, baptizing them in the name of the Father and the Son and the Holy Spirit. Teach these new disciples to obey all the commands I have given you. And be sure of this: I am with you always, even to the end of the age." Matthew 28:18-20 (NLT)

We have a tradition at our home. It started years ago. On Friday, if our grandson Strong is available, we have "BOYS' NIGHT OUT." Strong says, "It's Boys' Night Out but Mims can sleep there too."

Recently on one of our eventful sleepovers, I took Strong to the movie. While we were sitting in our seats at the theater, waiting for the movie to start, I asked Strong, "Why do you like Boys' Night Out so much?" Without hesitation came this response, "Because I can do anything I want to do." (We have tried to keep this a secret from his parents!)

Isn't it interesting that Jesus said, "The Father has given me all authority and I can do ANYTHING I want to do…and this is what I want…I want you to GO and MAKE DISCIPLES of all nations and baptize them and teach them the word of God and help them to walk in obedience to my Father's word."

Gary Keller has written in his book, *The One Thing*, to focus on the ONE THING that is most important in your life and whatever else happens… make sure you get that ONE THING done.

As you have walked through this 40 days we are coming to the end of the time that Jesus would spend on earth following His glorious resurrection on Easter Sunday. We are listening careful for our final instructions and now Jesus tells us, "I CAN DO ANYTHING I WANT TO DO BECAUSE I HAVE FULL AUTHORITY. WHAT I WANT TO DO IS TO SEND YOU INTO THIS WORLD TO MAKE DISCIPLES!"

YOUR NEXT DAY: Jesus has given you and me our "marching orders" and we are called to go into all the world and make Christ known. You may not travel overseas as a missionary but you can walk across the street as a neighbor. Think about your neighbors and identify one of them that you can invest in by sharing with them God's wonderful gift of eternal life made possible through the death and resurrection of Jesus Christ.

Day 38

NOTES about your Next Day

Day 39

"Could I Get Some Directions, Please?"

John 14:4-6

Cynthia always says the same thing when I am driving: "I don't know why you had GPS put in this car, you don't listen to the little lady in the dashboard telling you where to go any more than you listen to my directions."

She is not the only one that has expressed concern about my navigational ability. There was the time that I pulled across five lanes of interstate to make an exit in Chicago with Mike Jeffries in the car. I never knew Mike was Catholic but as we were sliding down the side of the off ramp he was yelling the name of Jesus and counting his beads. Then there was the time I traveled to Omaha with John Jones. I pulled out of the airport. John softly asks, "Do you know where you are going?" "No" I replied. "However I have discovered if you drive long enough you will eventually come to your destination." I was right. After 45 minutes, we had located our hotel. After our interview the next day we were checking out of our rooms and John said, "Do you know the fastest way to the airport?" The smart young clerk said, "Yes, sir! Just make a right out of our driveway and then left at the first light and you will be at the airport in about three minutes!"

Thankfully, when people start asking Jesus for directions to Heaven, the Master keeps it pretty simple.

"And you know the way to where I am going." "No, we don't know, Lord," Thomas said. "We have no idea where you are going, so how can we know the way?" Jesus told him, "I am the way, the truth, and the life. No one can come to the Father except through me." John 14:4-6

In life, sometimes directions can be very difficult, or they may be very easy and we are the ones that make them difficult. However, when Jesus was asked a direct question He gave Thomas a direct answer. There is only one way to heaven and that is through Jesus Christ.

YOUR NEXT DAY: If you have never trusted Christ as your personal Savior, take a moment right now and let me show you the way. Pray this simple prayer of faith: "Jesus, I need you in my life. I know that I have sinned and I know you died on the cross for my sin. I ask you to forgive me and I invite you by faith to come into my life. Thank you for the gift of eternal life. Amen!" If you do know Jesus, then write in your journal about when you gave your life to Him and followed His directions.

Day 39

NOTES about your Next Day

Day 40

"Heaven, We Have Liftoff!"

Acts 1:9-11

After saying this, He was taken up into a cloud while they were watching, and they could no longer see Him. As they strained to see Him rising into heaven, two white-robed men suddenly stood among them. "Men of Galilee," they said, "why are you standing here staring into heaven? Jesus has been taken from you into heaven, but someday He will return from heaven in the same way you saw Him go!" Acts 1:9-11 (NLT)

Our family had the wonderful privilege of pastoring at the First Baptist Church of Merritt Island in the height of the Space Shuttle launches. The NASA director was a member of our church and would invite us to sit in a VIP section where we would watch the giant countdown clock and then hear the powerful voice count down: "10-9-8-7-6-5-4-3-2-1 engines ignited, Houston, we have lift off!" The amazing power and force that you felt when the shuttle would take off is something you NEVER forget.

Two thousand years ago the disciples assembled on the launching pad on the Mount of Olives. It was a perfect day for the launch! It was a perfect view looking down from the mountain to see the entire city of Jerusalem below you. There were a few clouds on that day, but nothing that would threaten to stop the lift off. This launch had been planned since the beginning of time.

Jesus said His good-byes. He reminded His family and friends to remember what He had told them and then with absolute confident, divine knowledge…He took off, up, up, up into the clouds and his family and friends did just what our family would do at NASA: they strained their eyes tracing every movement as Jesus ascended into His Heavenly Home.

He continues to remind us from His word that "ALL SYSTEMS ARE GO" and He tells us that one day He will return and His return will be on the same mountain on which He left.

There are few things in life that are certain…this story is one of them. It has been a joy to travel with you these past forty days but it will also break my heart if you have not prepared for your trip into the heavenly realms. I want more than anything in this world to spend eternity, first with Jesus, then Cynthia and then our precious family and dear friends. Jesus has already made the trip with perfect success. All we have to do is follow Him. I will be with Jesus either when I die or when He comes back to get me.

Day 40, continued

Personally, either way is fine with me...I'm just looking forward to hearing that countdown:

"10-9-8-7-6-5-4-3-2-1! Larry has lifted off this old world and he is finally on the right course...headed to his home in Heaven. It was a PERFECT LIFT OFF. By the way, for those friends of Larry who are still on earth he wanted me to remind you to read John 3:16 to make certain you are ready for the flight. He said to tell you, he would be VERY disappointed if he doesn't get to spend eternity with you. He has some stories he couldn't tell you until you get there! So...Hurry Home!"

YOUR NEXT DAY: Finish your 40 days with Jesus by writing what your NEXT DAY is going to be like for you?

What has God called you to accomplish on your NEXT DAY?

Finally, write Him a thank you note for staying with us those 40 days after His resurrection and sharing with us such amazing spiritual truth.

Day 40

NOTES about your Next Day

Dedication

I started this journey as I contemplated the message God was giving me for our church on Easter Sunday. I realized Easter provided the entire world the hope of the NEXT DAY and for 40 days after His resurrection Jesus spent each day preparing all of us who are His followers for our NEXT DAY.

This book is dedicated to the most important NEXT DAYS in my life…

As a young man, my NEXT DAY was the most important of my life when I was introduced to the founder of the NEXT DAY, my risen Savior, Jesus Christ.

As a young college student, the NEXT DAY was Sunday and I sat by the most beautiful and godly woman I have ever known…43 years later and I still sit with the love of my life, Cynthia.

After over four years of marriage my wife gave me the news that the NEXT DAY we would discover that she was carrying our precious daughter, Taylor. Tay has become a NEXT DAY giant in our world, helping others less fortunate in our culture.

Two and half years later Cynthia would provide me with yet another NEXT DAY, when she introduced me to our second daughter, Jennifer. Jennifer made me laugh, and today as a professional, she continues to bring laughter back into the hearts of those whose lives have been broken.

It was the NEXT DAY that I became a father to sons, Mason and Marty. The world may call them son-in-laws but they will forever be my boys.

Then it happened, and the NEXT DAY I was introduced to my grandsons, Strong and Tru. It would be impossible to describe the joy of this NEXT DAY. I am sure there are Poppis out there that love their kids as much as I love mine…and if so, I know you understand my heart. I look forward to celebrating my grandson's NEXT DAYS as they carry the legacy of our family into their future.

The NEXT DAY a young journalism student walked into my office and said, "I want to help you." That young man, Mike Jeffries, has helped change my words and thoughts so that they actually make sense when others read them…more than editor and minister…he is my friend.

The NEXT DAY we moved to South Florida. We joined our hearts with this magnificent group of multi-cultural, multi-racial and multi-national followers of Jesus Christ. Little did I know that 21 years later, I would still have the honor of sharing life together with our amazing family at First Baptist Church of Fort Lauderdale.

Finally, I dedicate this book to all of you who will join with me in this NEXT DAY journey. I pray your NEXT DAY will bring the joy, peace and hope that EASTER SUNDAY has brought to this world.

About the Author

Dr. Larry L. Thompson has been senior pastor at First Baptist Church of Fort Lauderdale for more than twenty years, making him the longest-serving leader in the church's 100-year history. Pastor Thompson and his wife, Cynthia, have two daughters: Taylor (married to Martin Royle) and Jennifer (married to Mason Jones). They also have two grandsons, Strong and Tru.

Thompson's innovative methods feature a team approach to ministry which leads members in discovering their personal gifts, talents and passions to increase their effectiveness in helping others. With a background in theater and drama, Pastor Thompson is known as a dynamic, personable, practical communicator.

He led First Fort Lauderdale to complete construction of a 60,000-square-foot addition. This Community Life Center just east of the main Worship Center was built debt-free for $11 million contributed by church members and community friends. The expansion included a child development center, a global cafe and downtown's largest banquet center.

In 2006, Thompson received the National Conference on Community and Justice's Silver Medallion Award, presented to "individuals who have demonstrated leadership in promoting diversity and inclusiveness."

First Baptist Church of Fort Lauderdale is a unique church, having successfully transitioned from a traditional homogenous congregation to a multicultural community, with members from nearly 70 different nations. Weekly services are translated into five languages and transmitted live and on the Internet.

With a strong sense of the important experience of worship, Thompson's churches have been at the forefront of evangelical praise, recording two pacesetting projects from Integrity Music (*God With Us* and *Let His Glory Fall*, both with Don Moen). The *God With Us* project received the Gospel Music Association's Dove Award as "musical of the year."

At First Baptist Church of Merritt Island, Thompson co-authored a Christmas drama called Dickens' Christmas Journey with Reggie Joiner. More than three dozen churches have performed the original script.

First Fort Lauderdale hosts the Fort Lauderdale Christmas Pageant, a multi-million-dollar nationally televised holiday production. More than

50,000 South Florida residents make one of the Pageant's performances part of their Christmas season and special guests have included luminaries like Liza Minelli, Dan Marino, John Tesh and Don Shula. The Christmas Pageant has also been featured on ABC and Fox. Proceeds cover the cost of the event and benefit ministries around the world.

The Next Day is Pastor Thompson's fourth book. Dr. Thompson wrote *Hidden Heroes*, a book about unsung Biblical characters who achieved extraordinary accomplishments, and *Side by Side*, a devotional based on the book of Nehemiah. He developed the Watchman Prayer Ministry, an intercessory prayer program used in more than two thousand churches. The Watchman Prayer Ministry was also the cornerstone of the North American Mission Board's Watchman Alert national prayer strategy, which connected thousands of Christians in round-the-clock prayer. Pastor Thompson also developed the POP Strategy for outreach and wrote the accompanying booklet, *The Path*.

He received an honorary doctorate of letters from the University of Mobile for his efforts on behalf of international education and another from the California Graduate School of Theology for his work in church growth. He holds a master's degree from Luther Rice Seminary. Thompson has served on the Board of Trustees at the University of Mobile and Oklahoma Baptist University and was chairman of the board for the Little Lighthouse, a nonprofit school for the physically limited recognized by President George Bush with a "Thousand Points of Light" commendation. He helped organize and found the first U.S.-accredited university in Latin America.

Pastor Thompson has spoken on "The Circles of Change" at the Orange Conference and was selected as Pastor of the Year by the Fellowship of Christian Athletes. He has also been a seminar leader for the National Council on Creativity, a member of the resolutions committee for the Southern Baptist Convention and program speaker for the Southern Baptist Pastor's Conference.

He has three times received commendations from his home city of Fort Lauderdale, on the occasions of his tenth, fifteenth amd twentieth anniversaries as senior pastor at First Baptist Church.

His church sponsors more than two dozen missionary families, including the ongoing work at the Good Samaritan medical clinic and Carolina de Sirker schools in Nicaragua and homeless children's rescue shelters in Moscow and four other cities in Russia. His wife, Cynthia, serves as an adviser to the Jerusalem Prayer Center. In addition to extensive travels to Israel and Nicaragua, the Thompsons have participated in global mission endeavors in Haiti, Romania, Central Asia, and Jamaica.

Understanding "Reverse Lent" and the Church Calendar Year

Many Christian traditions celebrate *Lent*, the 40-day period preceding the events of Easter Weekend. This is a time of intense personal reflection, often emblemized by sacrificing something (like a favorite food or activity) for these 40 days.

Easter is a "moveable feast," meaning it moves on the calendar with the cycles of the moon and sun as God created them. Usually, Easter happens on the first Sunday after the first full moon after March 21.

While such pre-Easter introspection is important, perhaps it's even more important to reflect on our lives after the Easter Resurrection of Jesus. This is another Christian tradition, which seems to have been lost in many circles.

In the Church Calendar, every Sunday after Easter (until the Day of Pentecost) is known as "Easter Sunday." It's not just one particular Sunday morning when everyone dresses up, has an Easter ham and sends the kids searching for brightly colored eggs. For the earliest believers, the first of these "Easter Sundays" marked the promise and hope of a new beginning, but it was only a beginning. For the next seven Sundays, they would celebrate each "Easter Sunday" as a reminder of the new life they had been given in the Risen Savior.

This time period is called "Eastertide," named for that first Easter Sunday. Sundays of this season are called the Second Sunday of Easter, the Third Sunday of Easter all the way through the Seventh Sunday of Easter. In churches from the Eastern tradition, the 40 days between Easter and the Ascension of Jesus is called "Pascha."

This book is designed to recapture the Eastertide tradition with what we might term "reverse lent," with each of us being called to:
- reflect approaching Holy Week
- rejoice on the first Sunday of Eastertide
- renew our ways and live life more fully for Jesus in the 40 days after Easter and beyond

As you center your hopes on Jesus during these important seasons, we pray that these days from Easter to Easter will strengthen your relationship with God, your time with family and friends, and your connection with the world around us.

ENDNOTES

Preface
Alvin J. Schmidt, *How Christianity Changed the World*, (Grand Rapids: Zondervan, 2009), 137

Day 4
Edwin A. Blum, "John," John F. Walvoord (Editor), Roy B. Zuck (Editor), T*he Bible Knowledge Commentary: An Exposition of the Scriptures by Dallas Seminary Faculty [New Testament Edition]* (Colorado Springs: David C Cook Publishers), 341

Day 7
Alton Gansky, *Encounter Jesus Between the Resurrection and Ascension* (Nashville: B&H Press, 2007), 85

Day 8
Herschel Hobbs, *An Exposition of the Gospel of Mark* (Ada, MI: Baker Book House, 1970), 257

Day 10
Lee Strobel, *The Case for Christ: A Journalist's Personal Investigation of the Evidence for Jesus* (Grand Rapids: Zondervan), 1998, 237. Strobel's deep research is especially intriguing because of his experience as an investigative reporter for the *Chicago Tribune*.

Day 21
Videos of both S.M. Lockridge and Tony Campolo preaching "It's Friday, but Sunday's Comin'" are available on the Internet.

Day 33
World Christian Trends, Ad 30-Ad 2200: Interpreting the Annual Christian Megacensus , cited at https://compassioninpolitics.wordpress.com/2010/08/17/how-much-is-spent-on-christian-missions-each-year/

Day 24
Flavius Josephus, *Antiquities of the Jews*, Book 18, Chapter 3, 3, based on the translation of Louis H. Feldman, The Loeb Classical Library. http://www.josephus.org/testimonium.htm